BEAUTIFUL
Australia

BEAUTIFUL
Australia

*S*ydney is one of the world's great cities and is also Australia's largest. With its favourable climate and its location on the Harbour, Sydney has developed a comfortable lifestyle and a city-wide love affair with its waterways. The natural beauty of the city has been enhanced by the magnificent Harbour Bridge and Opera House, as well as by careful management of the city skyline.

*S*ydney, eine der bedeutendsten Städte der Welt, ist auch die größte Stadt Australiens. Seinem milden Klima und der Lage am Hafen verdankt es einen angenehmen Lebensstil, wobei die Einwohner die Wasserwege besonders lieben. Die prächtige Hafenbrücke, das Opernhaus sowie ihre im ganzen gutgeplante Silhouette heben die Schönheit dieser Stadt hervor.

*S*ydney est une des plus belles villes du monde, et la plus grande d'Australie. Grâce à son climat agréable et sa location dans le port, Sydney s'est créé un mode de vie aisé. Toute la ville est amoureuse de ses voies d'eau! La beauté naturelle de la ville est relevée par la splendeur de Harbour Bridge, l'Opéra, et par une ligne d'horizon qui a été méticuleusement soignée.

Left: *The Harbour Bridge and the Opera House, Sydney's two most famous landmarks.* Above: *Circular Quay, city terminal for the popular ferry services, is flanked by business towers and the beginning of the Harbour Bridge.* Below: *The Opera House on Sydney Cove, site of the first white settlement in Australia.*

Links: *Hafenbrücke und Opernhaus, die beiden berühmten Wahrzeichen Sydneys.* Oben: *Den Circular Quay, am Bahnhof des beliebten Fährbootverkehrs, umgeben aufragende Geschäftshäuser und die Einfahrt zur Hafenbrücke.* Unten: *Das Opernhaus in der Sydney Cove, wo die erste weiße Siedlung Australiens entstand.*

A gauche: *Harbour Bridge et l'Opéra, deux points de repères connus.* Ci-dessus: *Circular Quay, terminal des services populaires des 'ferry-boats', est flanqué d'immeubles commerciaux et Harbour Bridge.* Ci-dessous: *L'Opéra dans la baie de Sydney, lieu de la première colonie de blancs en Australie.*

Opposite, top: *Darling Harbour's shopping centre and the Novotel Hotel, reflected in the waters of Cockle Bay.* Opposite, bottom: *The Rocks, a very early settlement, has been restored as an historic and recreation area.* Right: *Skyscrapers tower over the wharves at Miller's Point.* Below: *Close to the central business district is the Darling Harbour Development, Sydney's latest entertainment, convention and exhibition centre.*

Gegenüber, oben: *Das Einkaufszentrum im Darlinger Hafen und das Novotel spiegeln sich im Gewässer der Cocklebai.* Gegenüber, unten: *The Rocks, eine der frühesten Niederlassungen, wurde vor der Zerstörung bewahrt und dient jetzt als Erholungsgebiet, das gleichzeitig von geschichtlichem Interesse ist.* Rechts: *Wolkenkratzer thronen über dem Kai am Miller's Point.* Unten: *In der Nähe des Geschäftsviertels befindet sich das Darling Harbour Development, Sydneys modernstes Unterhaltungs-, Konferenz- und Ausstellungszentrum.*

Ci-contre, en haut: *Le quartier commercial de Darling Harbour et l'hôtel Novotel sont reflétés dans les eaux de la baie de Cockle.* Ci-contre, en bas: *The Rocks, une colonie très ancienne, a été conservée et restituée en un lieu historique et de récréation.* A droite: *Des gratte-ciels dominent les quais à la pointe de Miller.* Ci-dessous: *Tout près du quartier commercial se trouve le développement de Darling Harbour, le nouveau centre de divertissement, d'exposition, et de salles de conférence à Sydney.*

Opposite, top: *As well as being a research institute of international repute, Sydney's Taronga Park Zoo occupies a prominent site on the Harbour's North Shore.* Opposite, bottom: *Bronte Beach, shown here, and Waverley have the oldest surf life-saving clubs in the country.* Above: *A timber surfboat, used by life-savers at Bondi, Sydney's most famous beach.* Right: *Sydney skyline, with South Head and the Harbour's North Shore in the foreground.*

Gegenüber, oben: *Sydneys weithin sichtbarer, am Nordufer des Hafen gelegener 'Tarongapark' beherbergt nicht nur den Zoo, sondern auch ein international anerkanntes Forschungsinstitut.* Gegenüber, unten: *Waverley sowie der hier abgebildete Bronte Beach verfügen über die ältesten Rettungsschwimmerklubs des Landes.* Oben: *Ein hölzernes Brandungsboot der Rettungsschwimmer von Bondi, dem berühmtesten Strand Sydneys.* Rechts: *Die Silhouette Sydneys mit dem South Head und dem Nordufer des Hafens im Vordergrund.*

Ci-contre, en haut: *Le Taronga Park Zoo de Sydney qui est situé bien en vue sur le Rivage du Nord de Sydney Harbour est aussi un institut de recherche de renommé internationale.* Ci-contre, en bas: *La plage Bronte, que l'on voit ici, et Waverley possèdent les plus vieux clubs de sauvetage de ressac au pays.* Ci-dessus: *Un bateau de surf en bois à Bondi, la plage la plus connue à Sydney.* A droite: *La ligne d'horizon de Sydney avec South Head et le Rivage du Nord de Sydney Harbour au premier plan.*

Above: *The beautiful south coast near Merimbula.* Left: *Homestead Gorge in Mootwingee National Park – typical of the Great Dividing Range which runs the length of Australia's East Coast.* Opposite, top: *Canberra's modern Parliament House on Capital Hill.* Opposite, bottom: *The Blue Mountains National Park near Sydney features the Bridal Veil Falls at Govett's Leap.*

Oben: *Die wunderbare Südküste in der Gegend von Merimbula.* Links: *Die Homesteadschlucht im Mootwingee-Nationalpark charakterisiert den Great Dividing Range, eine sich an der Ostküste Australiens erstreckende Gebirgskette.* Gegenüber, oben: *Das moderne Parlamentsgebäude thront auf Canberras Capital Hill.* Gegenüber, unten: *Die Bridal-Veil-Fälle am Govett's Leap befinden sich im Blue-Mountains-Nationalpark bei Sydney.*

Ci-dessus: *Le beau littoral du sud près de Merimbula.* A gauche: *La gorge de Homestead dans le parc national de Mootwingee est typique de la chaîne de montagnes le Great Dividing Range, située le long du littoral Est de l'Australie.* Ci-contre, en haut: *Le Parlement moderne de Canberra sur Capital Hill.* Ci-contre, en bas: *Le parc national de Blue Mountains près de Sydney a comme particularité les chutes de Bridal Veil à Govett's Leap.*

Opposite, top: *The Flinders Street Railway Station – a link with the past in the modern city of Melbourne.* Below: *The beautiful Yarra River is an important part of the city.* Right: *Melbourne landmarks – Princes Bridge, the Arts Centre and the Art Gallery beyond.* Bottom right: *Collins Street, the city's most famous thoroughfare, where elegant restaurants and boutiques alternate with pavement cafés.*

Gegenüber, oben: *Der Bahnhof Flinders Street verbindet die moderne Innenstadt Melbournes mit ihrer Vergangenheit.* Unten: *Der schöne Yarra River gehört einfach zum Stadtbild.* Rechts: *Melbournes Wahrzeichen – die Prinzenbrücke, das Kunstzentrum und dahinter die Kunstgalerie.* Rechts, unten: *In der Collins Street, der bekanntesten Durchfahrtsstraße der Stadt, wechseln sich elegante Restaurants mit Boutiquen und Straßencafés ab.*

Ci-contre, en haut: *La gare de la rue Flinders – un maillon avec le passé dans la ville moderne de Melbourne.* Ci-dessous: *La rivière Yarra représente dans sa splendour une partie intégrale de la ville.* A droite: *Des points de repères de Melbourne – le Pont des Princes, le Centre des Arts et au delà, la Galerie d'Art.* A droite, en bas: *La rue Collins, une voie dans la ville célèbre pour ses restaurants élégants, ses boutiques, et ses cafés trottoirs.*

Above: *The impressive Grampian Range –
popular holiday destination for walkers and climbers alike.*
Left: *At Black Spur, tall, straight eucalyptus trees tower
over the mountain road.* Opposite, top: *Grand country
hotels, such as this one in the historic town of Beechworth,
sprang up during the gold rush of the mid-nineteenth
century.* Opposite, bottom: *The Twelve Apostles, a
dramatic rock formation on the rugged coastline of Port
Campbell National Park.*

Oben: *Das beeindruckende Grampiangebirge,
Ferienziel für Wanderer und Bergsteiger.* Links: *Hohe
Eukalypten ragen über der Gebirgsstraße empor, Black
Spur.* Gegenüber, oben: *Vornehme Landhotels wie
dieses in der historischen Stadt Beechworth schossen
während des Goldrausches in der Mitte des neunzehnten
Jahrhunderts aus dem Boden.* Gegenüber, unten: *Die
Zwölf Apostel, eine imposante Gesteinsformation an der
zerklüfteten Küste des Port-Campbell-Nationalparks.*

Ci-dessus: *L'impressionnante chaîne de
montagnes Grampian – un lieu de vacances pour les
randonneurs et les ascensionnistes.* A gauche: *A Black
Spur, de grands et droits eucalyptus dominent la route
de la montagne.* Ci-contre, en haut: *De grandes auberges
de campagne, comme celle-ci dans le village historique de
Beechworth, ont été construites pendant la ruée vers l'or
au milieu du dix-neuvième siècle.* Ci-contre, en bas: *Les
Twelve Apostles, une formation rocheuse grandiose sur
la côte rugeuse du parc national de Port Campbell.*

Below: *Edged by mountains which are snow-capped for much of the year, Hobart, Tasmania, is Australia's second oldest and smallest state capital. A place of great natural beauty and quiet charm, it has a close and long-standing relationship with the sea (opposite, top). Right: The old part of Hobart nestles between the mountains, the sea and the Derwent River.*

Unten: *Fast das ganze Jahr hindurch sind die Berge schneebedeckt, die Hobart in Tasmanien umgeben. Australiens zweitälteste und kleinste Bundeshauptstadt erfreut sich landschaftlicher Schönheit und eines besonderen Reizes, der sich mit einer engen, langzeitigen Beziehung zum Meer verbindet (gegenüber, oben). Rechts: Die Altstadt Hobarts liegt zwischen Bergen, dem Meer und dem Derwent River eingebettet.*

Ci-dessous: *Entourée de montagnes qui sont enneigées la plus grande partie de l'année, Hobart en Tasmanie est la seconde plus ancienne et la plus petite capitale de l'état d'Australie. Un lieu d'une beauté naturelle, de charme, et de tranquillité, Hobart profite d'un rapport permanent avec la mer (ci-contre, en haut). A droite: L'ancienne partie de Hobart est nichée entre les montagnes, la mer, et la rivière Derwent.*

Below: *The rugged Tasmanian coastline is punctuated by peaceful fishing harbours such as Strahan. The Southern Ocean provides a rich fishing ground and supports a valuable local fishing and fish-processing industry.* Opposite, top: *Tasmania is studded with beautiful examples of colonial domestic architecture, such as Prospect House at Richmond.* Opposite, bottom: *An old colonial house stands in a dramatic river setting near Launceston, northern Tasmania.*

Unten: *Die zerklüftete Küste Tasmaniens wird von friedlichen Fischereihäfen wie Strahan unterbrochen. Die hiesige Fischerei ist von den ertragreichen Fischgründen des Südlichen Eismeers abhängig.* Gegenüber, oben: *Tasmanien ist von herrlichen Bauten der Kolonialarchitektur – wie Prospect House, Richmond – übersät.* Gegenüber, unten: *In einer imposanten Flußlandschaft steht dieses im Kolonialstil erbaute Haus bei Launceston, Nordtasmanien.*

Ci-dessous: *Le littoral rugueux de Tasmanie est accentué par des ports de pêche calms tel que Strahan. L'Océan du Sud est riche en poisson, et une importante industrie locale de pêche en dépend.* Ci-contre, en haut: *La Tasmanie est garnie de beaux exemples de maisons dans le style colonial, tel que Prospect House à Richmond.* Ci-contre, en bas: *Paysage théâtral: une ancienne maison coloniale construite près d'une rivière à Launceston, au nord de la Tasmanie.*

Above: *Cradle Mountain National Park in the interior of Tasmania, with its snow-covered peaks and clear streams, is a very popular attraction for bushwalkers. In the midst of the mountain lies Lake Dove* (right). Opposite: *Bird River in the beautiful southern part of the island, where rainforests, fast-flowing rivers and unspoilt ancient forests are found.*

Oben: *Den Cradle-Mountain-Nationalpark im Innern Tasmaniens mit seinen schneebedeckten Gipfeln und klaren Bächen wissen Wanderer besonders zu schätzen. In der Mitte dieses Berges liegt der Dovesee* (rechts). Gegenüber: *Bird River im südlichen Teil der Insel, wo man Regenwälder, schnellfließende Flüsse und vorzeitliche Wälder vorfindet.*

Ci-dessus: *Le parc national de Cradle Mountain à l'intérieur de la Tasmanie, avec ses pics couverts de neige et ses ruisseaux d'eau pure, est une attraction populaire pour les randonneurs de la brousse. Au milieu de la montagne se trouve le lac Dove* (à droite). Ci-contre: *La rivière Bird dans un coin magnifique du sud de l'île, où l'on peut trouver des forêts vierges, des rivières rapides, et des anciennes forêts non encore profanées.*

Opposite, top: *The old Adelaide Railway Station is one of several impressive late nineteenth century buildings on North Terrace.* Opposite, bottom: *Adelaide's skyline, seen across the historic cricket oval, the River Torrens and the Festival Centre.* Above: *The spires of St. Peter's Cathedral rise above the city's parklands in Montefiore Hill, a charming old suburb in North Adelaide.* Right: *The Chateau Tahbilk winery near Nagambie, whose cellar was built entirely from local materials.*

Gegenüber, oben: *Der alte Adelaider Bahnhof ist nur einer der eindrucksvollen, aus dem späten neunzehnten Jahrhundert stammenden Bauten der North Terrace.* Gegenüber, unten: *Blick auf Adelaides Silhouette über den historischen Kricketplatz, den Torrens River und das Festspielzentrum.* Oben: *In Montefiore Hill, einem alten Stadtteil Nordadelaides, überragen die Turmspitzen der Sankt-Peters-Kathedrale den Stadtpark.* Rechts: *Die Weinkelterei Chateau Tahbilk, deren Keller 1860 aus dem Baumaterial dieses Geländes erstellt wurde.*

Ci-contre, en haut: *L'ancienne gare d'Adelaïde est parmi les bâtiments les plus impressionnants de la fin du dix-neuvième siècle à North Terrace.* Ci-contre, en bas: *La ligne d'horizon d'Adélaïde, vue au-delà du terrain historique de cricket, de la rivière Torrens et du Centre des Festivals.* Ci-dessus: *Les flèches de la Cathédrale de St. Pierre s'élevant au dessus des parcs de la ville à Montefiore Hill, un vieux quartier plein de charme dans l'Adélaïde du Nord.* A droite: *Les caves du Château Tahbilk – le caveau a été construit en 1860 avec des matériaux provenant de la propriété.*

🇬🇧 Left, top: *King George Cove on the remote north coast of Kangaroo Island.* Opposite, bottom: *Australian sea lions perform at Seal Bay.* Above: *The Remarkable Rocks – Kirkpatrick Point in Flinders Chase National Park is scattered with these granite corestones, carved by nature into fantastic shapes.* Left: *South Australia's Barossa Valley was settled by German immigrants, who developed the area's wine-growing industry. The Immanuel Lutheran Church nestles in the vineyards at Light Pass.*

🇩🇪 Links, oben: *King George Cove an der abgelegenen Nordküste der Känguruhinsel.* Gegenüber, unten: *Australische Seelöwen bei einer Vorstellung in Sealbai.* Oben: *The Remarkable Rocks – aus den Granit-brocken am Kirkpatrick Point im Flinders-Chase-Nationalpark meißelte die Natur fantastische Gebilde.* Links: *Das südaustralische Barossatal wurde ursprünglich von deutschen Einwanderern besiedelt, die auch den Weinbau in diesem Gebiet entwickelten. Die Evangelisch-Lutherische Kirche Immanuel in Light Pass schmiegt sich an die Weinberge.*

🇫🇷 A gauche, en haut: *La baie King George sur la lointaine côte du nord de l'île Kangaroo.* Ci-contre, en bas: *Des otaries d'Australie jouent dans la baie de Seal.* Ci-dessus: *Les Remarkable Rocks – à la pointe de Kirkpatrick dans le parc national de Flinders Chase, ces pierres en granite, sculptées naturellement en des formes merveilleuses, sont éparpillées de toutes parts.* A gauche: *La vallée Barossa du sud d'Australie fut découverte par les immigrés allemands, qui ensuite développèrent la viticulture dans la région. L'Eglise luthérienne Immanuel à Light Pass est nichée dans les vignobles.*

Opposite, top: *South Australia's history has been marked by many settlers' abortive attempts to wrest a living from the land, as this domestic ruin in the Flinders Ranges testifies.* Opposite, bottom: *Dry as it is between heavy floods, northern South Australia supports vast flocks of birds, like these corellas.* Right: *In the north of the state, the desert landscape predominates.* Below: *The Nullarbor Plain ends abruptly at the craggy Bight Cliffs.*

Gegenüber, oben: *Die Geschichte Südaustraliens kennzeichnet viele erfolglose Versuche, sich in diesem Land einen Lebensunterhalt zu verdienen, dafür spricht diese Ruine im Flindersgebirge.* Gegenüber, unten: *Trotz der zwischen den Regenzeiten herrschenden Dürre leben im nördlichen Teil Südaustraliens zahlreiche Vögel, beispielsweise diese Kakadus.* Rechts: *Im Norden des Bundesstaates herrscht die Wüstenlandschaft vor.* Unten: *Die Nullarborebene geht jäh in die zerklüfteten Bight Cliffs über.*

Ci-contre, en haut: *Le passé de l'Australie Méridionale a été marqué par les tentatives manquées de plusieurs colons de cultiver à tout prix la terre, ce qu'en témoigne cette chaumière en ruines dans les montagnes de Flinders.* Ci-contre, en bas: *Même en temps de sécheresse entre les périodes de grandes inondations pluviales, le nord de l'Australie Méridionale parvient à subvenir à de nombreuses populations d'oiseaux, comme ces cacatoès.* A droite: *Au nord de l'état, le paysage désertique prédomine.* Ci-dessous: *La plaine Nullarbor s'arrête brusquement au pied de l'escarpement Bight Cliffs.*

Below: *Although Perth, capital of Western Australia, is isolated from the rest of the country, it has a modern city profile and an extensive network of expressways, while its riverside location and parks give the city a spacious feel. Opposite, top: Cyclists at King's Park, a great open space in the middle of Perth. Opposite, bottom: London Court, an Elizabethan-style shopping alley, is famous for the animated clocks found above each shop entrance.*

Unten: *Perth, die vom übrigen Land räumlich isolierte Hauptstadt Westaustraliens, verfügt doch über ein ausgedehntes Verkehrsnetz, während seine Lage am Fluß sowie die Parks den Eindruck der Weite vermitteln.* Gegenüber, oben: *Fahrradfahrer im Kingspark, den großzügigen öffentlichen Anlagen in Perths Stadtmitte.* Gegenüber, unten: *London Court, eine Einkaufspassage im elisabethanischen Stil, ist für seine über jedem Ladeneingang angebrachten Spieluhren bekannt.*

Ci-dessous: *Même si Perth, capitale de la province d'Australie Occidentale, est isolée du reste de l'Australie, elle ressemble à une ville moderne et possède un réseau étendu d'autoroutes alors que sa location en bordure d'une rivière et de parcs lui donne une sensation d'espace.* Ci-contre, en haut: *Des cyclists à King's Park, un grand espace au cœur de Perth.* Ci-contre, en bas: *London Court, une allée commerciale dans le style élisabéthain, est célèbre pour ses pendules animées situées a l'entrée de chaque magasin.*

Left: *The clear waters of Rottnest Island and the nearby mainland beaches attract many summer bathers. Close to Perth, the island and the city are linked by a ferry service.* Opposite, bottom: *Fremantle, the port of Perth, has retained many of its Victorian buildings, such as the Freemasons' Hotel of 1854.* Above: *Away from the city and the coast, though, Western Australia is a barren, sparsely populated area, which is rich in minerals but poor in soil quality and rainfall. Local fauna such as the wild camel, the wombat and the kangaroo constitute a driving hazard, as these road signs indicate.*

Links: *Das glasklare Wasser um Rottnest Island und die Strände des nahegelegenen Festlandes locken im Sommer Badegäste herbei. Zwischen dem nicht weit entfernten Perth und der Insel verkehren Fähren.* Gegenüber, unten: *In Fremantle, Perths Hafen, blieben zahlreiche viktorianische Gebäude, wie das Freemasons' Hotel aus dem Jahre 1854, erhalten.* Oben: *Fern der Städte und der Küste ist Westaustralien ein dürres, kaum besiedeltes Land, reich an Bodenschätzen, doch unfruchtbar und niederschlagsarm. Die einheimische Fauna – das Wilde Kamel, der Wombat und das Känguruh – gefährden, wie diese Schilder zeigen, den Verkehr.*

A gauche: *Les eaux claires de l'île Rottnest et, non loin de là, les plages du continent, attirent les baigneurs d'été. Près de Perth, l'île et la ville sont reliées par le ferry.* Ci-contre, en bas: *Fremantle, le port de Perth, a conservé plusieurs de ses bâtiments victoriens, comme l'hôtel Freemasons, construit en 1854.* Ci-dessus: *Loin de la ville et de la côte, l'Australie Occidentale est une région aride et peu peuplée. La terre est riche en minéraux mais elle est de mauvaise qualité et il y a peu de précipitations. La faune du pays, tels que le chameau sauvage, le phascolome et le kangaroo, constituent des hazards routiers, comme l'indiquent ces panneaux.*

Opposite, top: *Cottesloe Beach is cooled by the wind known as the 'Fremantle Doctor'.* Left: *Proximity to the sea is no guarantee of fertile land, as the arid Cape Naturaliste National Park shows, but for all its barrenness, the park is a place of rare beauty and tranquillity.* Above: *In the great semi-wilderness of the state's interior is the unique geological formation of Wave Rock at Hyden.*

Gegenüber, oben: *Den Cottesloe Beach kühlt ein als 'Fremantle-Doktor' bekannter Wind.* Links: *Die Nähe des Meeres gewährleistet keineswegs die Fruchtbarkeit des Bodens, das erkennt man an der Öde des Cape-Naturaliste-Nationalparks. Trotz aller Trostlosigkeit überwältigt einen die seltene Schönheit und Stille dieses Gebiets.* Oben: *Der Wave Rock bei Hyden zeigt beispielhaft die einzigartigen geologischen Formationen der Halbwüste im Innern Westaustraliens.*

Ci-contre, en haut: *La plage de Cottesloe est rafraîchie par un vent connu sous le nom du 'Docteur Fremantle'.* A gauche: *La proximité de la mer ne donne pas de garanties pour une terre fertile, comme le démontre l'aridité du parc national du Cap Naturaliste, mais malgré toute sa sécheresse, le parc est exceptionel par sa beauté et son calme.* Ci-dessus: *Au milieu du grand semi-désert à l'intérieur se trouve l'unique formation géologique de Wave Rock à Hyden.*

Above: *Western Australia presents a wide array of unusual geological features, such as the Pinnacles.* Left: *Feeding fish at Coral Bay – one of the many pleasures of this state's immensely long shoreline.* Opposite, top: *In the Kimberley region of the north lie the unruffled waters of the Lower Manning Gorge, and a series of monoliths at Purnululu (Bungle Bungle) National Park* (opposite, bottom) *shows the red stain of the iron that is so important in the geology of the state.*

Oben: *Westaustralien verfügt über vielfältige, außergewöhnliche geologische Wahrzeichen, wie die Pinnacles.* Links: *Beim Füttern der Fische in der Korallenbucht – eine der vielen Freuden, die diese ausgesprochen lange Küstenlinie bietet.* Gegenüber, oben: *Im Norden, im Umkreis Kimberleys, breitet sich das stille Gewässer der Lower-Manning-Schlucht aus, während die rote Färbung einer Gruppe Monolithen im auch als Bungle Bungle bekannten Purnululu-Nationalpark auf das Eisen deutet, das für die Geologie dieses Bundesstaates so wichtig ist* (gegenüber, unten).

Ci-dessus: *L'Australie Occidentale offre un déploiement de formes géologiques inhabituelles telles que les Pinnacles.* A gauche: *Des enfants donnent à manger aux poissons à la baie de Corail – un des nombreux plaisirs côtiers de ce rivage immense et long.* Ci-contre, en haut: *Dans la région de Kimberley située dans le nord, les eaux calmes de la gorge de Lower Manning, et une série de colonnes monolithes au parc national de Purnululu (Bungle Bungle) montre le coloris rouge du fer qui se trouve en grande quantité dans la composition géologique du pays* (ci-contre, en bas).

Above and opposite, top: *Uluru (formerly known as Ayers Rock), the great landmark and major attraction of Australia's 'Top End', is the world's biggest single monolith. Left: Alice Springs, the Northern Territory's second largest city, is the stepping-off place for Uluru and other natural features of central Australia, such as the Devil's Marbles (opposite, bottom).*

Oben und gegenüber, oben: *Uluru (früher hieß es Ayers Rock), der weltweit größte Inselberg, gilt am 'Oberen Ende' Australiens als besondere Sehenswürdigkeit. Links: In Alice Springs, der zweitgrößten Stadt des Nordterritoriums, finden Gäste Unterkunft, die den Uluru und andere, in Mittelaustralien gelegene Naturdenkmäler, wie Devil's Marbles (gegenüber, unten), besuchen wollen.*

Ci-dessus et ci-contre, en haut: *Uluru (appelé autrefois Ayers Rock), le fameux point de repère et la grande attraction du 'Top End' d'Australie, est la colonne monolithe solitaire la plus grande du monde. A gauche: Alice Springs, la deuxième plus grande ville du Territoire du Nord, est un relais pour Uluru et d'autres attractions naturelles du centre de l'Australie, telles que les Devil's Marbles (ci-contre, en bas).*

Far left: *The Kakadu National Park draws visitors from across the country and abroad.* Opposite, bottom: *Aborigines gathered for a corroboree at Mandora.* Above: *The interior of the Northern Territory is a strange and lonely place with many unusual features, like this termite mound.* Left: *Venturing off the few paved roads in the Northern Territory demands care and the proper equipment, such as a four-wheel drive.*

Ganz links: *Der Kakadu-Nationalpark zieht Besucher aus ganz Australien und aller Welt an.* Gegenüber, unten: *Aborigines treffen sich bei Mandora zum 'Corroboree'.* Oben: *Im Landesinnern besticht das Nordterritorium durch seine Eigenart und Einsamkeit, dafür zeugt u.a. dieser Termitenhügel.* Links: *Wer sich von den wenigen befestigten Straßen im Nordterritorium wagt, braucht außer Vorsicht auch die richtige Ausrüstung, z.B. ein Fahrzeug mit Vierradantrieb.*

Plus loin à gauche: *Le parc national de Kakadu attire les visiteurs du pays et d'outre-mer.* Ci-contre, en bas: *Une réunion rituelle d'aborigènes à Mandora.* Ci-dessus: *L'intérieur du Territoire du Nord est un endroit singulier et isolé possédant plusieurs particularités étranges, comme cette termitière.* A gauche: *S'aventurer en dehors des rares routes goudronnés dans le Territoire du Nord demande de la vigilance et un équipement convenable, tel que le quatre-quatre.*

Above: *Brisbane, set on the Brisbane River and Morton Bay, is the capital of Queensland and Australia's third largest city. Opposite, bottom: The Gold Coast's white beaches attract millions of visitors each year. Right: The Sunshine Coast's climate, favourable all year round, has made it a tourist Mecca, with the apt slogan, 'beautiful one day, perfect the next'. Noosa, shown here, is one of its centres.*

Oben: *Brisbane, die Hauptstadt von Queensland und Australiens drittgrößte Stadt, liegt am Brisbane River und an der Mortonbai. Gegenüber, unten: An die weißen Strände der Goldküste strömen jährlich Millionen Besucher. Rechts: Da das Klima an der Sunshine Coast das ganze Jahr hindurch angenehm ist, entwickelte sich hier ein wahres Mekka für Besucher, die dem durchaus angebrachten Motto des Gebiets vertrauen: 'Ein Tag wunderschön, der andere perfekt'. Das hier abgebildete Noosa zählt zu den hiesigen Kurorten.*

Ci-dessus: *Brisbane, située le long de la rivière Brisbane et la baie de Morton, est la capitale de Queensland et la troisième plus grande ville d'Australie. Ci-contre, en bas: Les plages blanches de la côte Gold attirent des millions de visiteurs par an. A droite: Le climat sur la côte Sunshine, qui est agréable tout le long de l'année, a transformé cet endroit en une 'Mecque' de tourisme. Et son slogan bien adapté: 's'il fait beau aujourd'hui, il fera encore plus beau demain'. Noosa, que vous voyez ici, est un de ses centres commerciaux.*

Above: *Just north of Noosa lies Fraser Island. The world's largest sand island, it has a number of fresh-water lakes such as Lake Wabby. Most travel occurs on the flat, level beaches* (left). Right: *The Hayman Island Resort is located on the popular Whitsunday Islands, just off the mainland coast.* Opposite, bottom: *Mooloolaba on the Sunshine Coast.*

Oben: *Im Norden von Noosa liegt Fraser Island, die größte Sandinsel der Erde. Hier befinden sich einige Süßwasserseen, wie der Wabbysee. Als Verkehrswege dienen vorwiegend die flachen, geraden Strände* (links). Rechts: *Der Ferienort Hayman Island liegt unmittelbar vor der Festlandküste auf den beliebten Whitsunday Islands.* Gegenüber, unten: *Mooloolaba an der Sunshine Coast.*

Ci-dessus: *Juste au nord de Noosa se trouve l'île Fraser. La plus grande île constituée de sable au monde, elle a aussi plusieurs lacs d'eau douce tel que le lac Wabby. On se déplace le plus souvent sur les plages plates et nivelées* (à gauche). A droite, en haut: *La station balnéaire de l'île Hayman est située sur les fameuses îles de Whitsunday, toutes proches de la côte du continent.* Ci-contre, en bas: *Mooloolaba sur la côte Sunshine.*

Above: *A small boat takes tourists through the crystal-clear waters of the Great Barrier Reef, near Lady Musgrave Island.* Opposite, left: *A reminder of years gone by is found in the impressive Cairns Post Office, which was built in 1882.* Opposite, right: *Road travel in northern Queensland is not without its hazards – one must be aware, it seems, of possums, emus, kangaroos and bush fowl of all kinds!* Above, right: *Visitors flock to Palm Cove near Cairns, the largest city of far northern Queensland.*

Oben, links: *Ein kleines Boot mit Touristen bei Lady Musgrave Island auf dem kristallklaren Wasser des Great Barrier Reef.* Gegenüber, links: *An die gute alte Zeit in Cairns erinnert das eindruckvolle, im Jahre 1882 erbaute Postamt.* Gegenüber, rechts: *Autoreisen im Norden von Queensland sind nicht ganz ungefährlich, es scheint fast so, als müsse man auf Opossums, Emus, Känguruhs und Buschhühner jeglicher Art achten!* Oben: *Besucher strömen in Scharen nach Palm Cove bei Cairns, der größten Stadt im Norden Queenslands.*

En haut, à gauche: *Une embarcation amenent des touristes dans les eaux claires du Great Barrier Reef, près de l'île de Lady Musgrave.* Ci-contre, à gauche: *Un souvenir du passé se trouve au Bureau de Poste de Cairns, construit en 1882.* Ci-contre, à droite: *Prendre la route dans le nord de Queensland n'est pas sans danger – on dirait qu'il faut faire attention aux opossums, aux émeus, aux kangaroos et à toutes sortes d'oiseaux de la brousse!* En haut: *De nombreux visiteurs affluent à la baie de Palm, près de Cairns, la plus grande ville au nord de Queensland.*

Above: *With the Great Barrier Reef, tropical rainforests and islands, golden beaches and blue waters, Queensland's coastline is a holiday destination without peer.* Left: *Not all of Queensland is a coastal paradise, however, as these red sand dunes at Windorah show.* Opposite, top: *North of Cairns lies the Daintree Forest, one of the state's most beautiful and important rainforests.* Opposite, bottom: *The Glasshouse Mountains in the south are visible from afar.*

Oben: *Das Great Barrier Reef, tropische Regenwälder und Inseln, goldene Strände und blaues Meer – Queenslands Küste ist ein Urlaubsziel ohnegleichen.* Links: *Doch nicht ganz Queensland besteht aus einem Küstenparadies, das bezeugen diese Dünen bei Windorah.* Gegenüber, oben: *Nördlich von Cairns liegt der Daintree Forest, einer der herrlichsten und bedeutendsten Regenwälder des Bundesstaates.* Gegenüber, unten: *Die Glasshouseberge im Süden nimmt man bereits aus großer Entfernung wahr.*

Ci-dessus: *Avec le Great Barrier Reef, des forêts vierges, des îles, des plages dorées, et des eaux bleues, le littoral de Queensland est une destination sans égal pour les vacanciers.* A gauche: *Ce n'est pas le paradis côtier partout à Queensland comme le démontrent ces dunes rouges à Windorah.* Ci-contre, en haut: *Au nord de Cairns se trouve la forêt de Daintree, une des forêts vierges la plus belle et la plus grande de l'état.* Ci-contre, en bas: *Les montagnes Glasshouse dans le sud sont évident de loin.*

Above: *It is difficult to exaggerate the appeal of the Queensland coast – so well illustrated here by a spectacular sunrise at Palm Cove, Cairns.*

Oben: *Der Reiz der Küste Queenslands läßt sich kaum übertreiben – das veranschaulicht der Sonnenaufgang in Palm Cove, Cairns.*

Ci-dessus: *Il est difficile d'exagérer le charme de la côte de Queensland – tellement évident ici avec le lever du soleil dans la baie de Palm, à Cairns.*

Published by National Book Distributors and Publishers Pty Ltd
Unit 3/2 Aquatic Drive, Frenchs Forest, NSW, 2086, Australia

First edition 1994

Text © Laurie Ryan

Design concept Neville Poulter
Design and DTP Lyndall Hamilton
Cartography Globetrotter Travel Map
Editor Jenny Barrett
French translator Agnès Bouchardeau
French editor Dana Mills
German editor Gudrun Grapow

Reproduction by Hirt & Carter (Pty) Ltd, Cape Town
Printed and bound by Kyodo Printing Co. (Pte.) Ltd, Singapore

**National Library of Australia
Cataloguing-in-Publication data**
Ryan, Laurie
Beautiful Australia
ISBN 1 86436 005 4

Photographs © individual photographers and/or their agents as follows:

Auscape International p 40 (bottom); **ATC** p 29 (top and bottom right), p 30 (bottom); **Ross Barnett** p 6 (top), p 7 (top), p 9 (bottom), p 10 (bottom), p 11 (bottom), p 14 (top), p 15 (top), p 22, p 23 (top), pp 24-25; **Donna Browning/Auscape International** front cover (middle inset), p 38 (bottom); **John Carnemolla/APL** p 7 (bottom); **Roger du Buisson** p 12 (top); **Jean-Paul Ferrero/Auscape International** p 43 (top); **Darran Leal/Auscape International** back cover, p 44 (top); **J Marks/APL** p 8 (bottom); **Larry Mulvehill** p 9 (top); **Nick Rains** front cover (main photograph), title page, pp 4-5, p 6 (bottom), p 10 (top), p 13 (bottom right), p 14 (bottom), p 15 (bottom), pp 16-18, p 19 (bottom), p 20 (bottom), p 21 (bottom), p 23 (bottom), p 26 (bottom), p 27 (bottom), p 30 (top), p 31, p 32 (top), p 33 (top), p 34 (bottom), p 35 (bottom), p 36 (top), p 37 (top), p 42 (bottom), p 46 (bottom); **Nick Rains/APL** p 27 (top), p 28, p 32 (bottom), p 34 (top), p 35 (top), p 41 (bottom), p 42 (top), p 43 (bottom), p 47 (bottom); **Paul Steel** front cover (left inset), pp 2-3, p 11 (top), p 12 (bottom), p 13 (top), p 19 (top), pp 20-21 (top), p 26 (top), p 36 (bottom), p 37 (bottom), p 38 (top), p 39, p 40 (top), p 44 (bottom left and right), p 45 (right), p 46 (top), p 47 (top), p 48; **Taronga Park Zoo** p 8 (top); **Dave Watts/National Photographic Index** front cover (right inset).